Contents

2	Introduction/The Romans
4	Lincoln 30 CE
6	Lincoln 60 CE
8	Lincoln 150 CE
10	Lincoln 250 CE
12	The Legionary Fortress
14	The Upper Colonia *(city)*
16	The Lower Colonia *(city)*
18	Newport Arch
20	The Forum and Basilica
22	The Fortuna Mosaic
24	The Townhouse Mosaic
26	The Ninth Legion
28	The Horse Brooch
30	The Horkstow Mosaic
32	Roman Lincoln today

Symbols used in this guide

Outlines of Roman walls
(still visible)

Roman points of interest
(still visible)

Lincoln Museum

Outlines of Roman walls
(no longer visible)

Roman points of interest
(no longer visible)

Roman Lincoln looking north, 250 CE.

Introduction

The area where Lincoln is located was occupied for around two centuries before the Roman invasion. This was part of the territory of the *Corieltavi*[1] tribe, long established in the East Midlands region, but not hostile to the Roman invaders. The Roman occupation and growth of the city is the focus of this guide, exploring the period from 50 CE to 350 CE. After this date the Roman Empire started a gradual decline and by 410 CE Britain was under constant attack by marauding Anglo-Saxons. The guide brings to life how Lincoln could have looked, with full-colour images all looking north *(unless indicated otherwise)*, reconstructions of artefacts, and detailed maps showing where each site is in present-day Lincoln.

1. There are slightly different spellings of Corieltavi, Corieltauvi, or Coritani. Corieltavi is thought to loosely mean 'Land of many rivers'.

Towns and cities

The Romans defined towns and cities differently to how we do in the present day. They had three main types of town:
- *A Colonia, which was a rough equivalent of a city.*
- *A Municipium, which was slightly less important than a colonia.*
- *A Civitas capital, which was a broad equivalent of a large market town.*

The Romans called Pre-Roman towns 'oppida'.

The Romans

The city of Rome in central Italy was formed around 800 BCE and grew over the centuries into the Roman Empire, which covered most of Europe and northern Africa. It was a highly sophisticated and technologically advanced society, with a huge army, major roads and large cities. Britain at that time was a mysterious place with fierce tribes and valuable metals, which became the focus of an attempted invasion in 55 BCE and 54 BCE by *Julius Caesar*. Those invasions were repelled by local tribes and the Romans did not try again to invade Britain for almost 100 years. By 43 CE the *Emperor Claudius (who needed the army's support)* decided to invade Britain, focusing his initial attack on the south-east of England. By 50 CE Roman forces were moving across the East Midlands to occupy the area where Lincoln now stands...

Visiting Lincoln

Lincoln lies about 120 miles (193 km) north of London. The main museum showing Roman Lincoln in depth is the Lincoln Museum, which was a Roman Townhouse and is now home to a large number of Roman artefacts and exhibits. Remains of the Roman city walls and gates, and partial remains of other Roman sites, can be seen around the city.

Lincoln looking north, 30 CE.

Lincoln 30 CE

Before the Roman invasion Lincoln was part of the territory of the *Corieltavi* tribe, which covered most of modern Leicestershire, Nottinghamshire and Lincolnshire. Their main tribal centres were at Leicester, 56 miles *(90 km)* south-west and Old Sleaford, 20 miles *(32 km)* to the south. A small Iron Age settlement near modern Lincoln was clustered around a lake[1] in the marshy floodplain of the River Witham, with a steep hill close by and with a river connection to the North Sea. The Romans recognised the strategic advantages of the site as a military base, but it is thought that the *Corieltavi* valued it for spiritual rather than military reasons, as a place of sacred water. Many precious objects were deposited in the area as ritual offerings over the centuries before the Roman invasion. The Celtic name for this place was *'Lindon'*, meaning *'the pool/lake'*; later the Romans called it *'Lindum'*.
1. *Present day Brayford Pool, see right.*

Find out more
Brayford Pool, on Lincoln's modern waterfront, is located to the south of the city centre. The expanse of water would have been much larger before the Romans arrived, and covered with marshland.

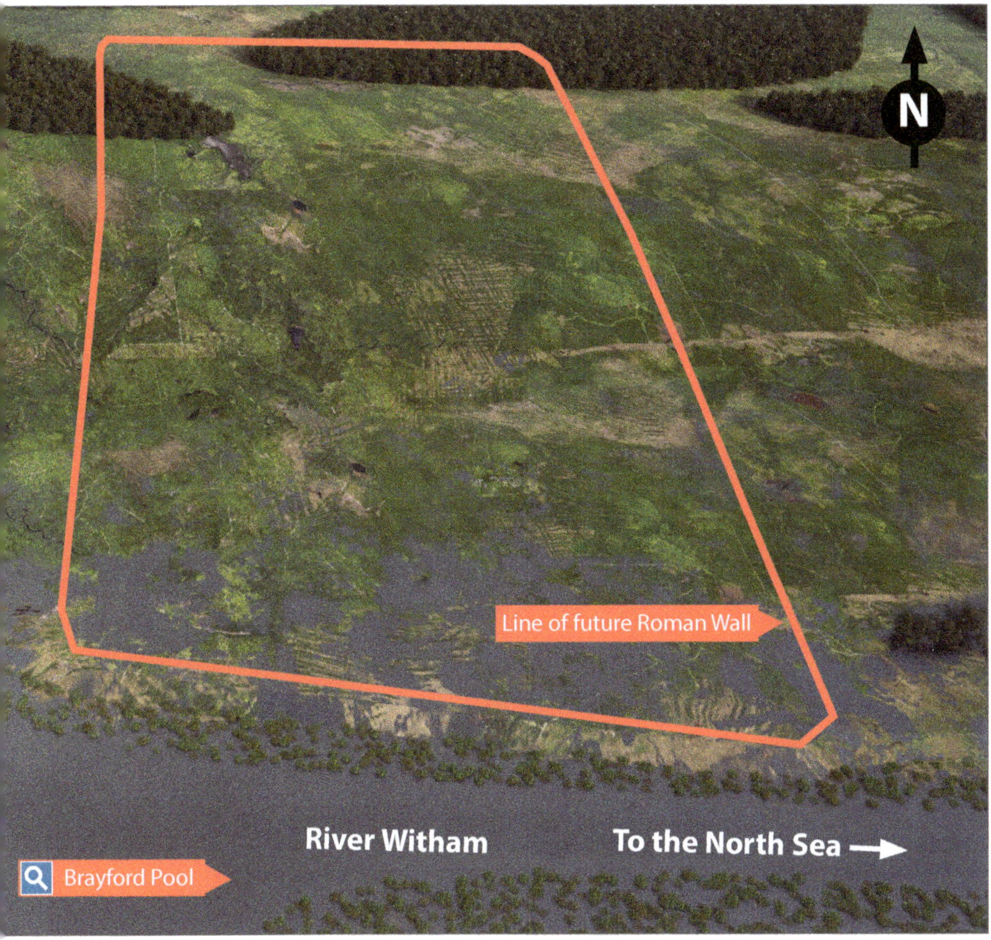

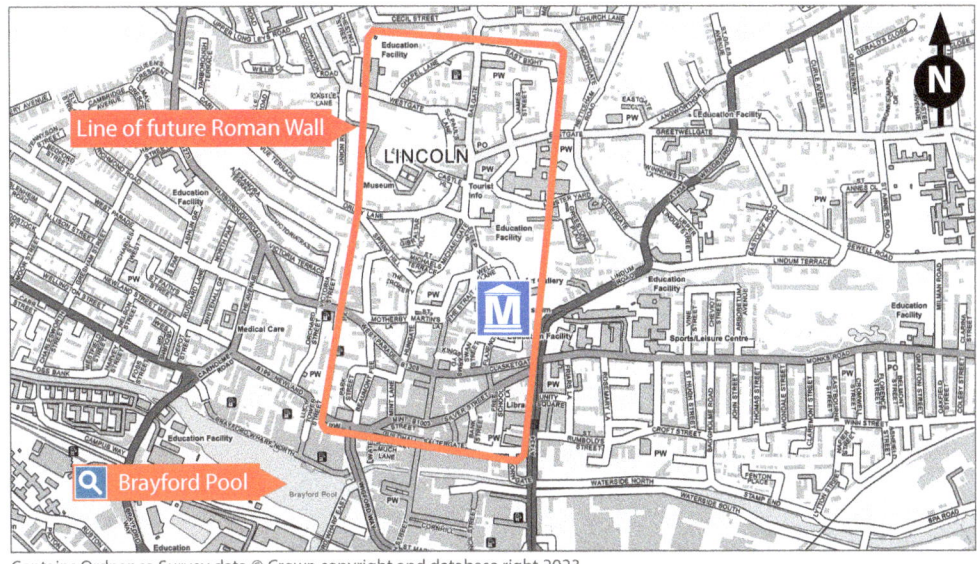

Lincoln looking north, 60 CE

Lincoln 60 CE

As part of the Romans' advance north they laid out major roads: Fosse Way from Exeter *(via Leicester)*, and Ermine Street from London. The site of Lincoln was where the two key roads met, making it a good place to site a legionary fortress around 47 CE, built by the *Legio IX Hispana (Ninth Spanish Legion)*. The steep hill would have been a strategic vantage point, with the river giving them access to supplies from the North Sea[1]. Around 60 CE a permanent fortress was built at the top of the hill, with defensive ditches and turf ramparts. Ermine Street was its main road, running from south to north through the centre of the fortress. The *Corieltavi* seemed to have welcomed the Romans, as protection from their aggressive neighbours, the *Brigantes*.

1. The Romans had a large navy, known as Classis Britannica, which in part supplied the Roman Army and also patrolled the North Sea and English Channel.

Find out more
Medieval Lincoln Castle is built directly over the south west corner of the Legionary Fortress. Some remains are visible in the castle. The line of the original defensive ditches and gates can be seen in the medieval city walls. The Principia (the administrative hub of the fortress) in later years became the Forum and Basilica (see page 20).

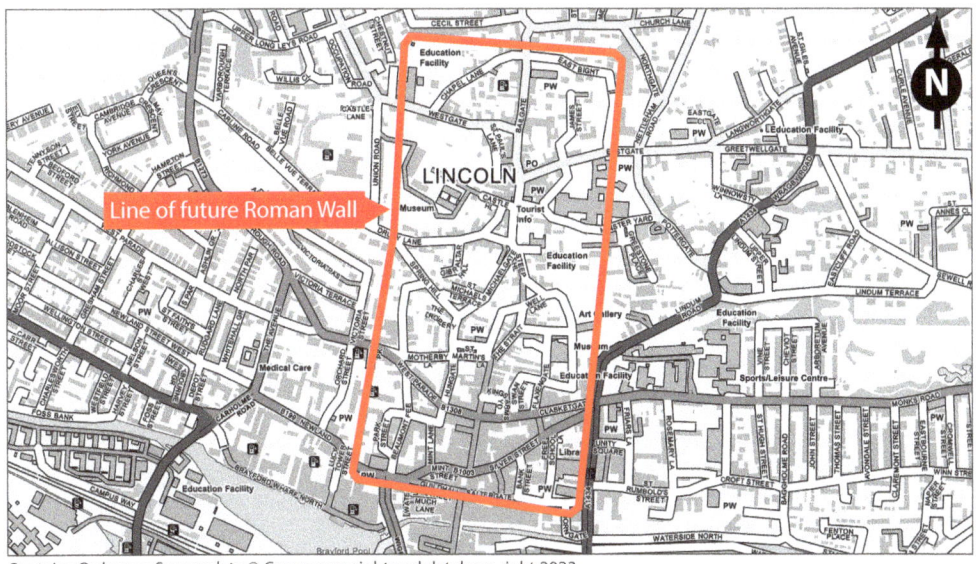

Lincoln looking north, 150 CE.

Lincoln 150 CE

By 70 CE the *Legio IX Hispana (Ninth Spanish Legion)* were sent north to establish a new fortress at York. *Legio II Adiutrix (Second Legion, Supporter)* took their place, but also not for long; they were redeployed outside Britain by 78 CE. Lincoln[1] became a colonia around this time *(see page 14)*, and was no longer a military base. The original timber walls and gates were reinforced with stone, and large public buildings replaced the military headquarters. Grand townhouses were being built here too, for a growing civilian population. The area was very steep at the top of the hill, so the Romans constructed terraces. They also constructed the Fossdyke Canal, enabling merchants to send their barges inland to the River Trent, as well as along the River Witham to the North Sea and beyond.

1. Lincoln's offical Roman name was Colonia Domitiana Lindensium, or Lindum Colonia for short.

Find out more

Many sections of the wall and gates are still visible, also parts of the forum complex (see page 20). The Fossdyke Canal, thought to have been built by the Romans, is still used today. The outline of a 2nd century Castellum Aquae (watertank) can be seen just east of Newport Arch, which most probably connected to one of the aqueducts which supplied the colonia. The Fosse Way and Ermine Street merge just south of Lincoln city centre.

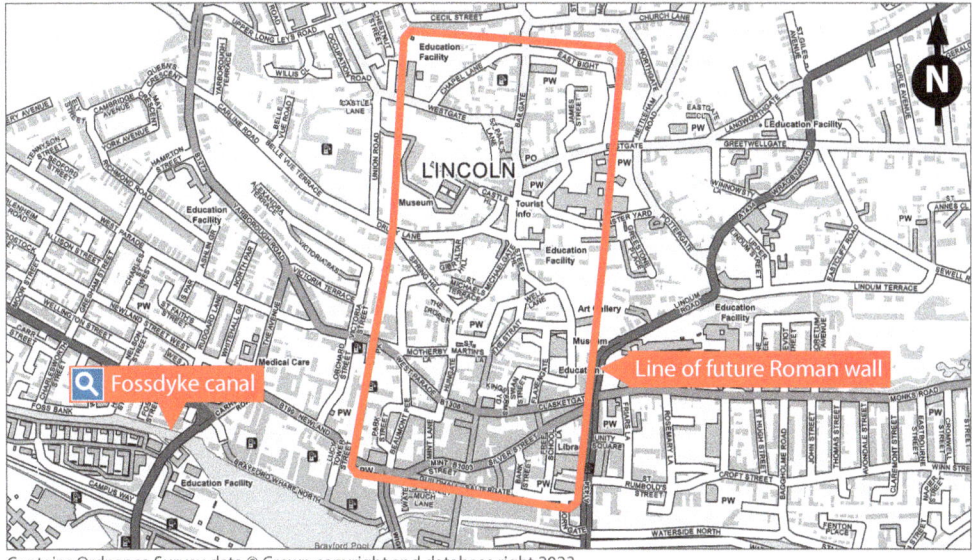

Lincoln looking north, 250 CE.

Lincoln 250 CE

Over time the colonia expanded downhill, eventually doubling the size of the original city. The *'downhill'* section was commercial and industrial, in contrast to the grand civic centre in the upper town. The defences of the upper town were strengthened around this time, including Newport Arch and the other three main gateways. The upper southern gateway was particularly impressive, halfway up Steep Hill. A wall was built to enclose the lower town and protect the important waterfront area, with a postern gate giving direct access for merchants using the waterfront. It is thought a large theatre was built on the terraces overlooking the terraces. Pantomimes were more popular than plays, as well as comedies based on people's lives.

After the Romans
By the time the Vikings attacked around 865 CE, Lindum Colonia (Lincoln) was then known as Lincylene.

Find out more
The main outline of Lindum Colonia is shown in red on the map, key sites are described in the following pages. Small parts of the Colonia wall still survive, as shown on the map. It would have stood about 4 metres (13 feet) high and been about 4 metres (13 feet) wide, although by 250 CE it was up to 7 metres (22 feet) high. Along with seven gatehouses and the 4th century Posterngate, (leading to the river) there were around 40 towers defending the colonia.

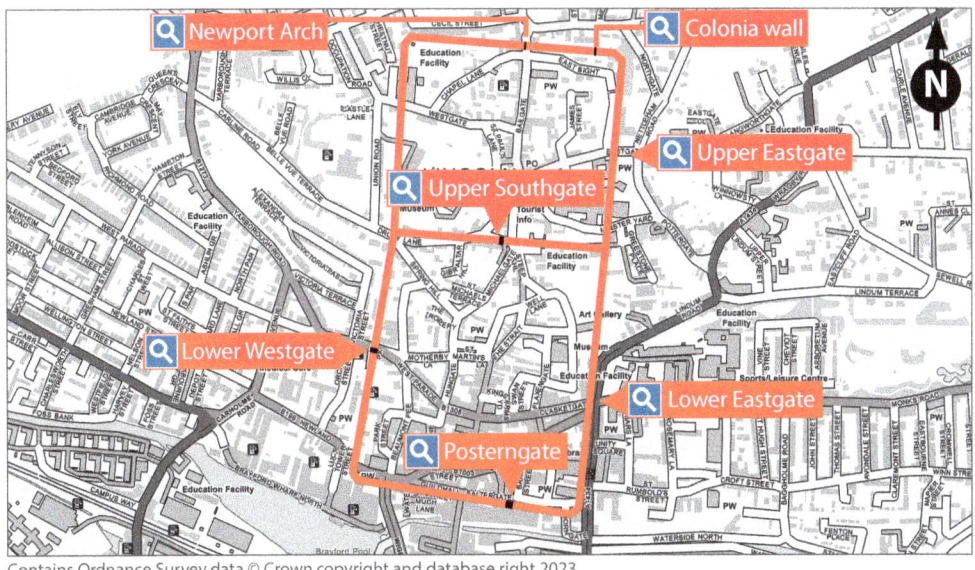

The Legionary Fortress looking north, 60 CE. Some of the buildings are conjectural.

The Legionary Fortress

One of the first tasks for the soldiers constructing the Legionary Fortress in 60 CE was to build its defences. They dug out ditches surrounding the fortress to stop it being overrun, and used the soil from the ditches to add height to a wooden palisade *(defensive wall)*. It would have had wooden watchtowers along with gatehouses, to allow the soldiers patrolling the perimeter to have clear views into the surrounding countryside. Like most Legionary Fortresses, Lincoln followed a standard design of a rectangle with rounded corners. Inside the walls were the Principia *(headquarters building[1])*, and other buildings. The *Legio IX Hispana (Ninth Spanish Legion)*, who built the fortress around 60 CE, constructed a well 15 metres *(49 feet)* deep, to supply fresh water for the 5000 soldiers based there.

1. By 90 CE this had become the Forum and Basilica.
2. The Praetorium was the residence of the military commander.

Find out more

There are no parts of the fortress visible, except for the well at the bottom of Bailgate, as they would have been built from wood, and were later built over in stone when the fortress became the upper part of the Colonia (see overleaf). The fortress wall and Newport Arch would also have been built from wood, but were also upgraded later with stone, some of which can be seen in the present day.

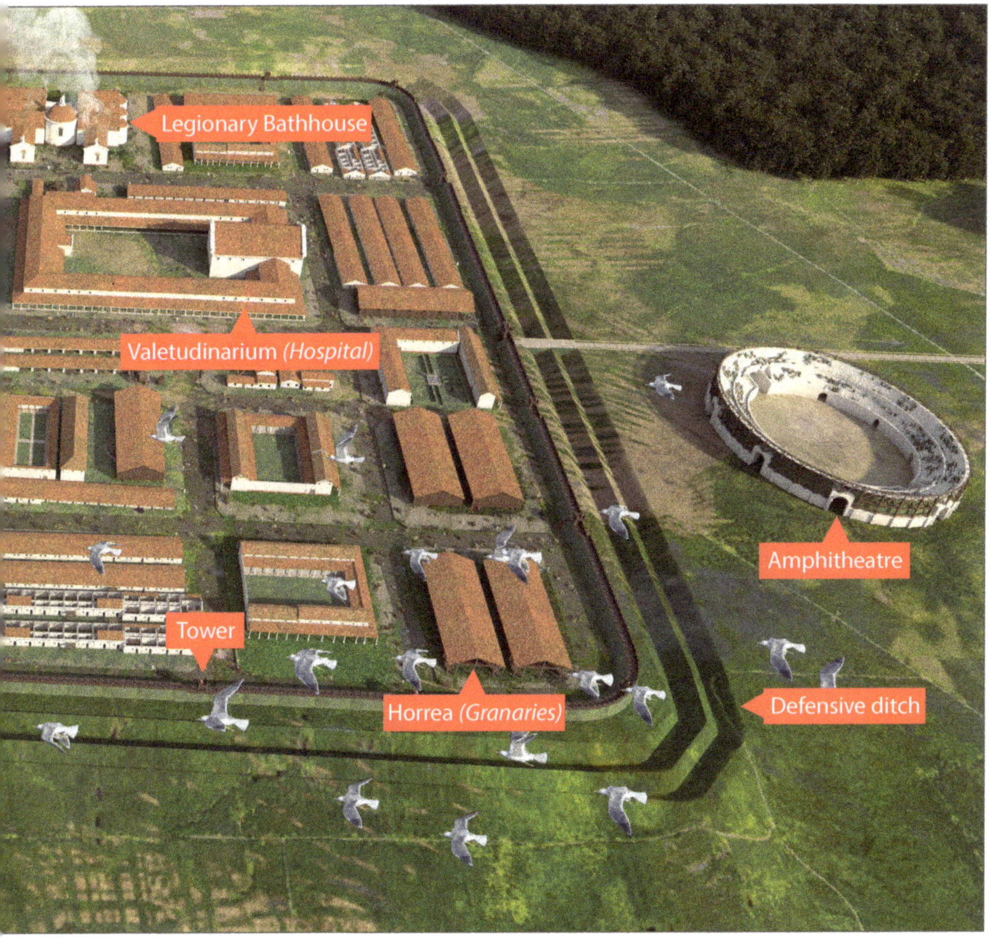

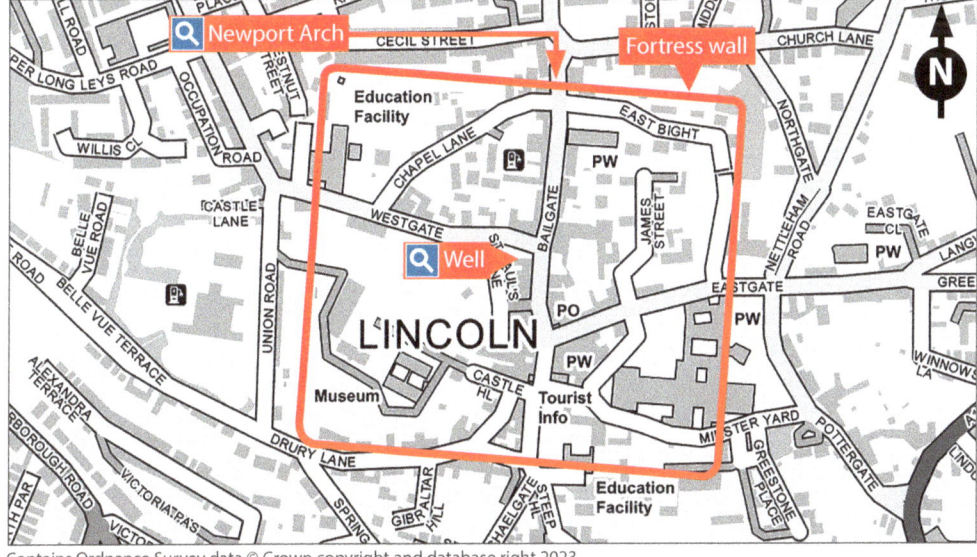

14. The Upper Colonia (city)

The Upper Colonia looking north, 250 CE. The site of the amphitheatre is speculative.

The Upper Colonia *(city)*

Lincoln was granted colonia status around 89 CE. This was the highest legal status for a Roman city in Britain; only four were created *(the others were Colchester, Gloucester and York)*. It meant that civilian Lincoln could be self-governing, with a council made up of veteran soldiers and prominent local citizens. A colony of veteran soldiers was established in a walled area on the upper slopes of Steep Hill *(originally the site of the Legionary Fortress)*, gradually expanding into a second walled area further downhill *(shown overleaf)*. Lincoln's citizens built imposing public buildings, especially the Forum, with the Basilica *(administrative centre)* as its civic centre, replacing the Fortress's Principia. Other public buildings included temples and public bathhouses. The area between the Fortress and Colonia was so steep that terraces had to be constructed to allow houses and possibly a theatre to be built, as well as steps leading to Upper Southgate.

Find out more

Originally the site was the Legionary Fortress, shown earlier, which became the Upper part of the Colonia. There are many parts of the Upper Colonia which can be seen in the present day, as shown on the map, including: Newport Arch, parts of the Forum and parts of the wall. Evidence of two temples has also been found, one dedicated to Apollo (the god of truth and healing) and one dedicated to Mercury (the god of communication).

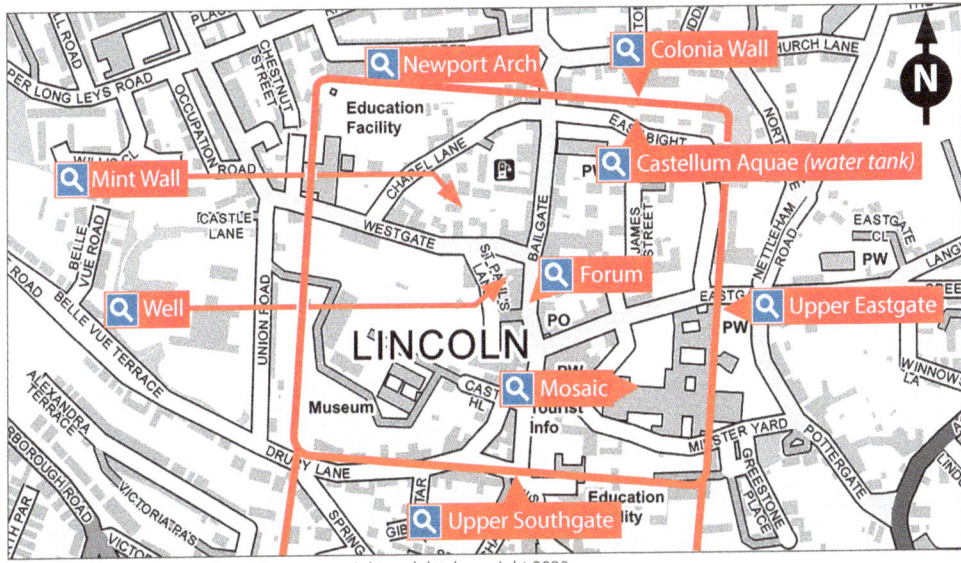

16. The Lower Colonia (city)

The Lower Colonia looking north, 250 CE. The sites of the macellum and Triumphal Arch are speculative

The Lower Colonia *(city)*

While the original Upper Colonia was the Legionary Fortress, the Lower Colonia had originally been a collection of market stalls and small houses lining Ermine Street *(which led from London to York via Lincoln)*. This area or *Vicus (equivalent to a village)* over the decades became the Lower Colonia. Public buildings as in the upper city were built, such as temples, bathhouses and a public fountain. By 250 CE the area had a defensive wall with gatehouses including a new Southgate and the small Posterngate. This led out to the waterfront where items from all over the Empire had been transported by riverboats. Some of these included cattle for market and wine from Bordeaux. It seems that the wealthy and powerful lived in the Upper Colonia, while the Lower Colonia was the industrial area of Lincoln. Here would have been a high concentration of markets and workshops rather than the large townhouses found in the Upper Colonia.

Find out more

The Posterngate was a 4th century gate added to the wall, there are limited tours available (see online). A small section of the Colonia Wall and 4th century defensive ditch can be seen in the Temple Gardens. Motherby Hill follows the general line of the Colonia Wall on the west side; although no actual remains are visible, archaeologists found pottery and part of a tower. A quite hard to find section of the Westgate can be found in 'The Park'.

Theatre
Terracing
Lower Eastgate
Public Bathhouse
Defensive ditch
Colonia Wall
Posterngate
N

Upper Southgate
Motherby Hill
Colonia wall
Ditch
Lower Westgate
Lower Eastgate
Posterngate
N
Education
Art Gallery
Medical Care
Education Facility
Library
Museum
SPRING HILL
ST MICHAELS TERRACE
THE EROPERY
MOTHERBY LA
ST MARTIN'S LA
WEST PARADE
HUNGATE
B1308
CLASKETGATE
CARHOLME ROAD
B199 NEWLAND
BRAYFORD WHARF NORTH
PARK STREET
BEAUMONT FEE
MINT LANE
MINT STREET
SILVER STREET
GUILDHALL STREET
SALTERGATE
MUCH LANE
FREE SCHOOL LA
UNITY SQUARE
FRIARS LA
ROSEMARY LA
ST RUMBOLD'S STREET
A1434
WHITEHALL GR
RUDGARD LANE
DEPOT STREET
VICTORIA STREET
LUCY TOWER STREET
WELL LANE
PW

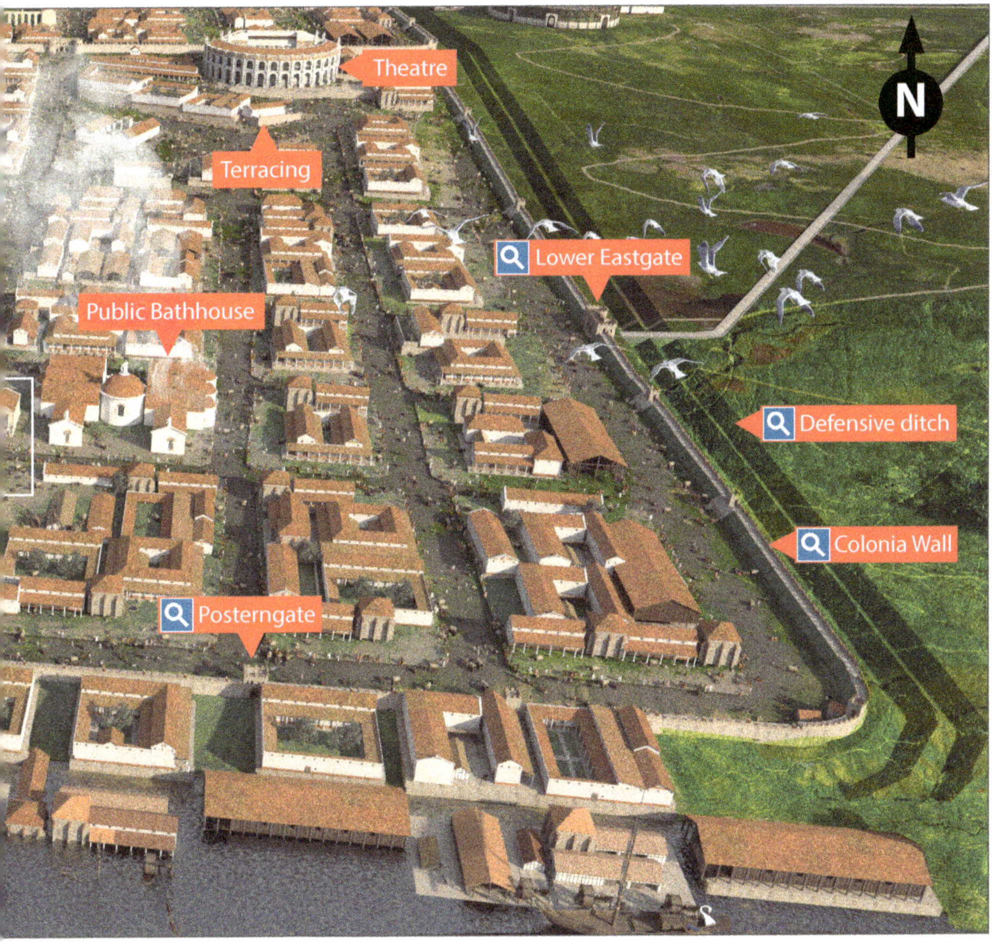

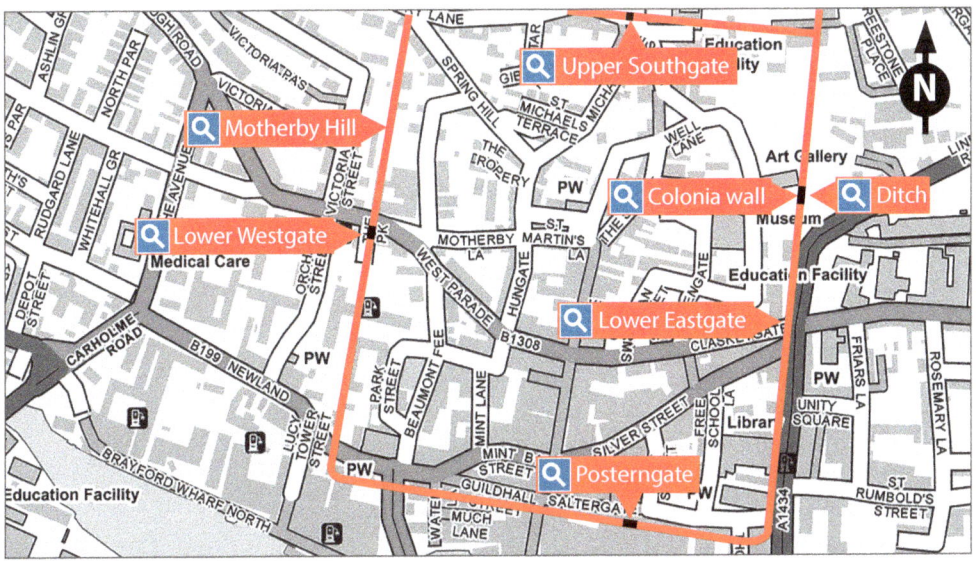

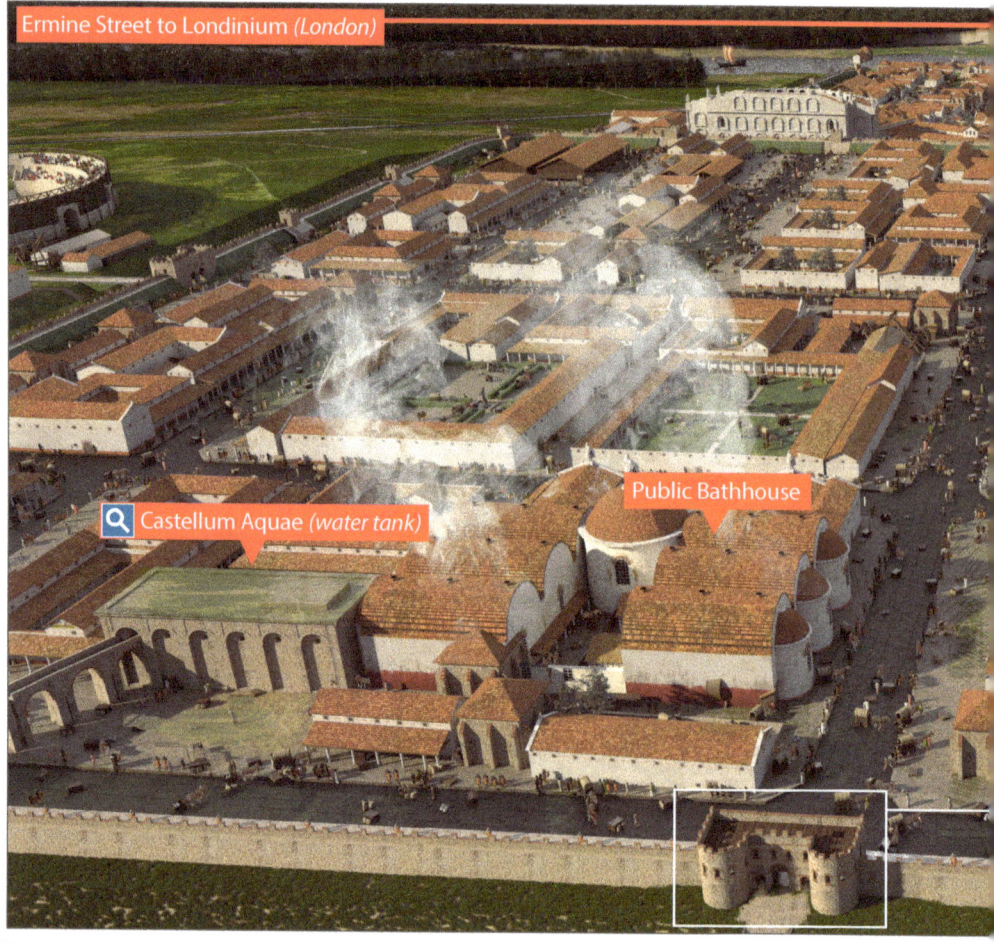

*Newport Arch looking **south**, 250 CE.*

Newport Arch

Newport Arch was Lincoln's north gate, one of the four original fortress gates. It formed the northern entrance to the upper city along the important Roman road Ermine Street linking London to York, which ran through the centre of Lincoln. This would have been a strategic control point on the route that the legions and their military supplies would take to and from northern Britain. At first Newport Arch would have been constructed from timber around 55 CE, but when Lincoln became a colonia around 89 CE it was rebuilt in stone. It was rebuilt again in the third century, this time as a massive monumental gateway, built to impress. It had a single central arch wide enough for wheeled carriages, with pedestrian archways on either side. Archaeologists in 1954 recorded that the gate was actually much taller than it is now, with the modern ground level almost 3 metres *(10 feet)* higher than in Roman times.

Find out more

Newport Arch is still the northern entrance to the city centre, the only surviving Roman gateway with road traffic passing through it in daily use in Britain. Only its inner arch remains, with the complete eastern pedestrian arch and part of the western pedestrian arch. The outer parts were demolished around 1790. It probably acquired its name in medieval times as the gate leading to the suburb of Newport.

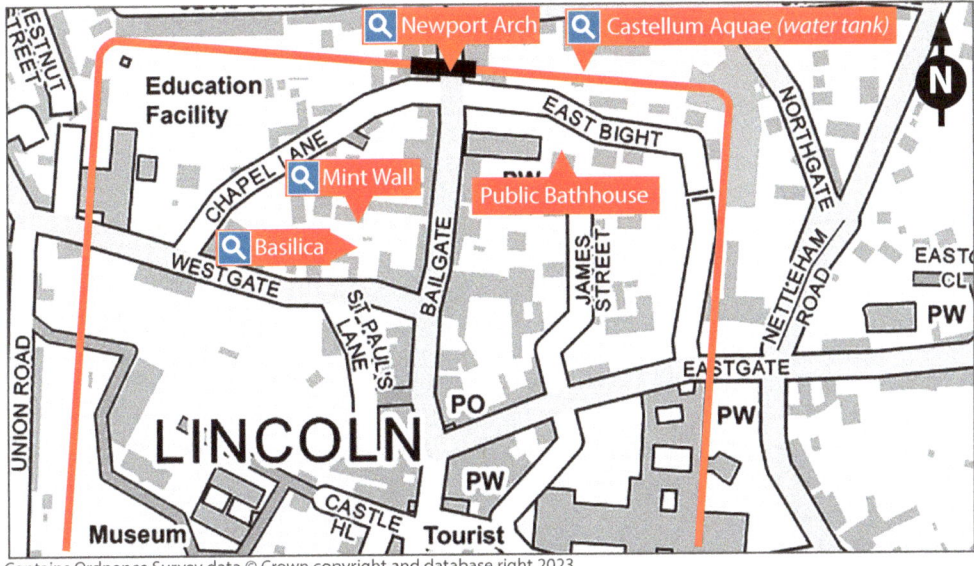

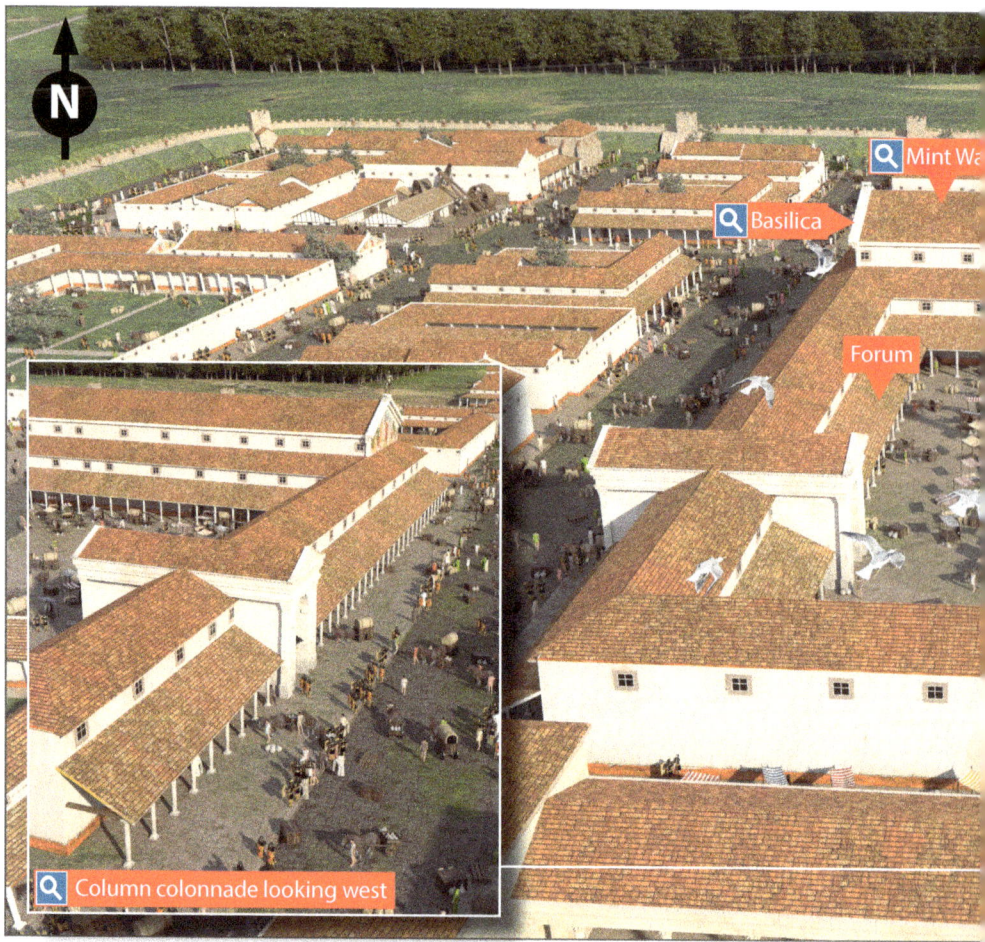

The Forum and Basilica looking north, 250 CE.

The Forum and Basilica

The Forum *(public square)* and Basilica *(hall)* were built over the site of the fortress Principia[1]. The Basilica was the commercial and administrative heart of Lindum Colonia, and was where deals were made and laws practised; it was also the regional government office. Large statues would have dominated the Forum where the population of the local area could meet. Various offices for local administrators and merchants surrounded the Forum, which had a large double colonnade providing shade in summer and shelter in winter. There was a covered well at its centre *(originally the Fortress Well)*, and there would also have been market stalls selling food and household items sourced from all over the Roman Empire. Some of the merchants who traded here became very rich and built large villas in the surrounding fertile countryside.

1. The Forum and Basilica may have been built around 90 CE.

Find out more

Much of the site is hidden beneath Lincoln Cathedral. The Mint Wall, a huge section of Roman wall 6 metres (19 feet) high and 20 metres (65 feet) long, is all that can now be seen of the Basilica. The only visible remains of the Forum are the well (still visible in Bailgate) and the traces of colonnade columns, indicated in the pavement of modern Bailgate. The outline of a possible 4th century Roman church can be seen near to the well.

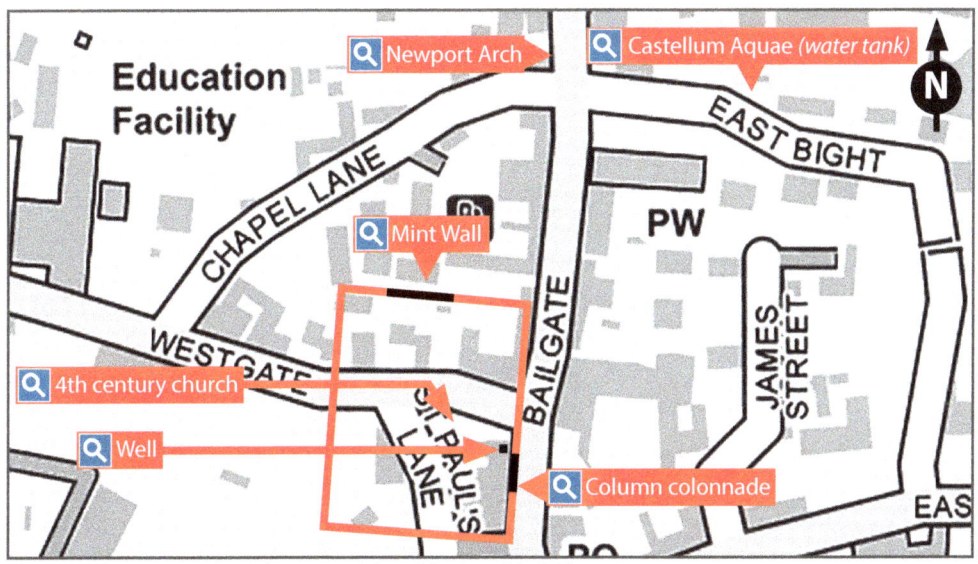

A speculative interior of the office which may have housed the Fortuna Mosaic, around 250 CE.

The Fortuna Mosaic

In 1897 excavations in the area where the Forum was located unearthed part of a mosaic, which is thought to either represent *Fortuna*[1] or one of the seasons[2].

It probably was much larger and may have formed the floor of one of the offices which surrounded the Forum.

Around the figure is a circular border of guilloche[3] pattern framed by a simple edging of red and white tesserae and decorations of lotus flowers and hearts.

1. Fortuna was the Roman goddess of fortune, luck and fate.
2. The seasons (Spring, Summer, Autumn, and Winter) feature on some mosaics in Roman Britain, such as the spectacular one on display in Cirencester.
3. Guilloche are interweaving patterns, commonly found on Roman mosaics, which were thought to represent infinity.

Find out more

The Fortuna mosaic can be seen in the Lincoln Museum. The image is a speculative view of how the mosaic **may** have looked. 'Summer' is suggested here, with the other seasons, rather than Fortuna.

A view showing how much of the mosaic can be seen in the present day.

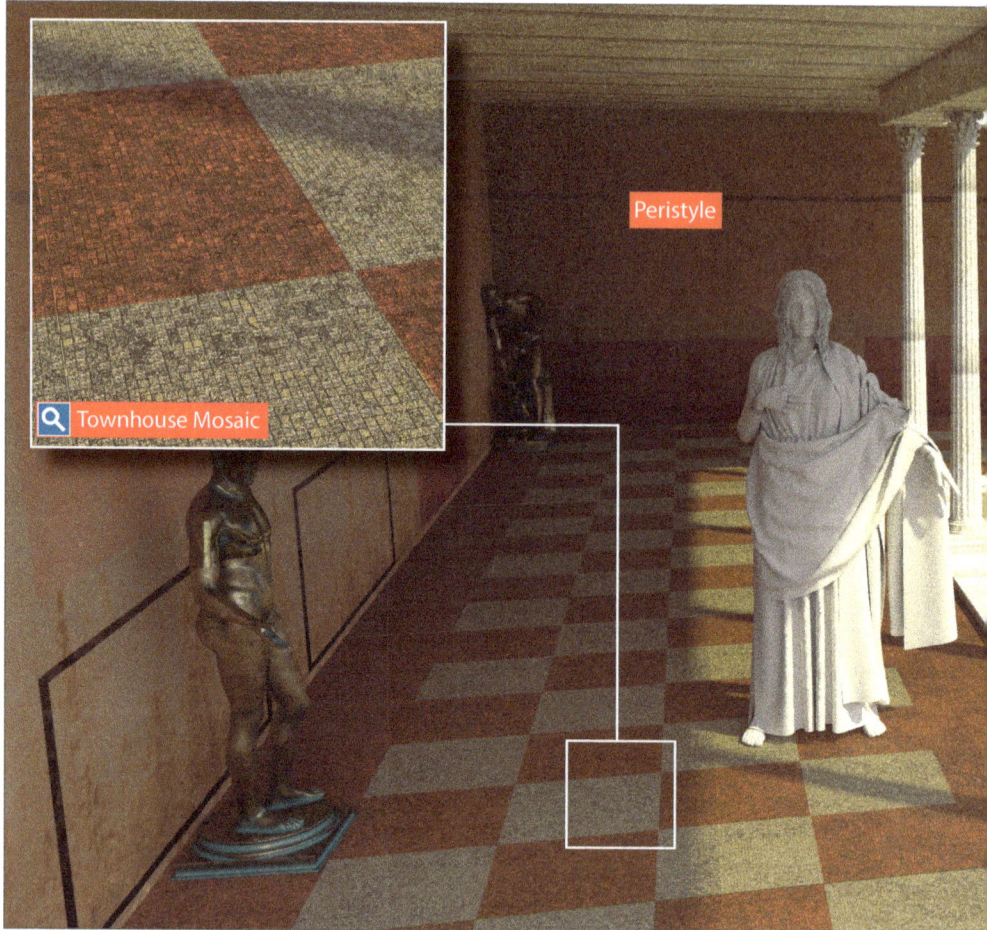

A possible exterior view of the Townhouse Mosaic, around 350 CE.

The Townhouse Mosaic

Beneath the Lincoln Museum lies a fourth-century Roman townhouse, discovered when the museum was under construction in 2003. An L-shaped mosaic corridor from the townhouse is still in exactly the same place as when the townhouse's Roman occupants walked across it almost 1,700 years ago. The layout of a townhouse such as this would have had courtyard spaces away from the noise of the city outside, and with more complex mosaics in the main reception rooms. Its owners may have been wealthy merchants, as this part of the city was in the commercial and industrial zone below the grander district at the top of Steep Hill. Here they may have entertained guests such as wealthy merchants or politicians, while walking around the *peristyle (continuous porch)* admiring the *hortus (garden)*. These types of gardens were ornamental, full of flowers, shrubs and ornate statues.

Find out more

The Townhouse Mosaic can be seen beneath the floor of the Lincoln Museum. There are digital displays of the townhouse, allowing visitors to take a virtual tour. You can also see examples of Roman roof tiles, as shown top right, in the Lincoln Museum. The main image shows a few of the plants which were brought to Britain by the Romans, such as box.

A view showing how much of the mosaic can be seen in the present day.

A view showing typical weapons and equipment used by the Ninth Legion.

The Ninth Legion

The *Legio IX Hispana (Ninth Spanish Legion)*, which established the fortress at Lincoln, was one of the original four legions which invaded Britain in 43 CE. After the invasion they fought native tribes in the west and built Lincoln's fortress around 50 CE. The Ninth Legion was to suffer devastating losses trying to relieve Roman forces fighting *Boudica* and her 120,000 *Iceni* warriors at Colchester in 60-61 CE. By 71 CE the Ninth Legion had moved on from Lincoln to establish the fortress at York after defeating the local *Brigantes*, but were to just escape destruction from a night attack by forces in Caledonia *(present day Scotland)*. What happened to them after that is something of a mystery, the last known record of them was at York. Some think they were wiped out after 108 CE in Caledonia, while others believe they were wiped out possibly in Judea *(present day Palestine/Israel)* or Armenia.

Find out more

The Lincoln Museum has many artefacts from the Ninth Legion. They include an inscription commemorating a legionary standard-bearer, Gaius Valerius. He was known to be a native of Italy. Other soldiers in the Ninth Legion who were based in Lincoln came from Macedonia and Spain.

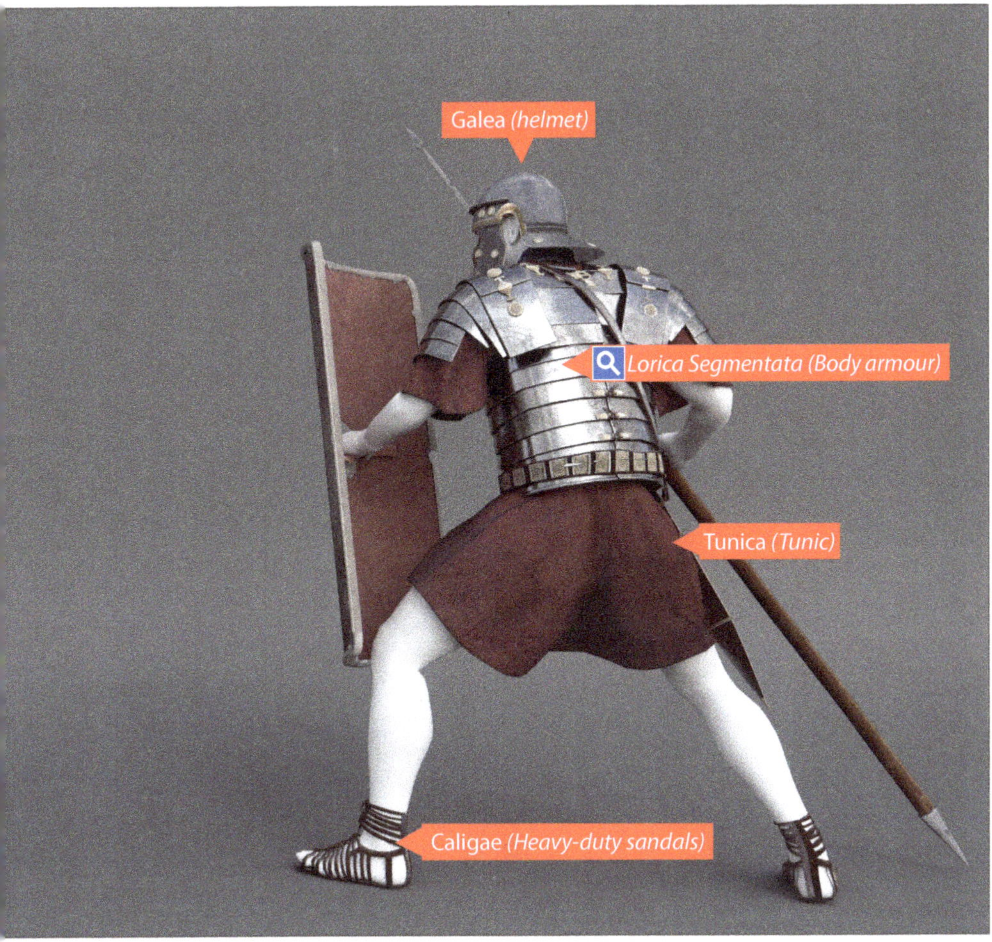

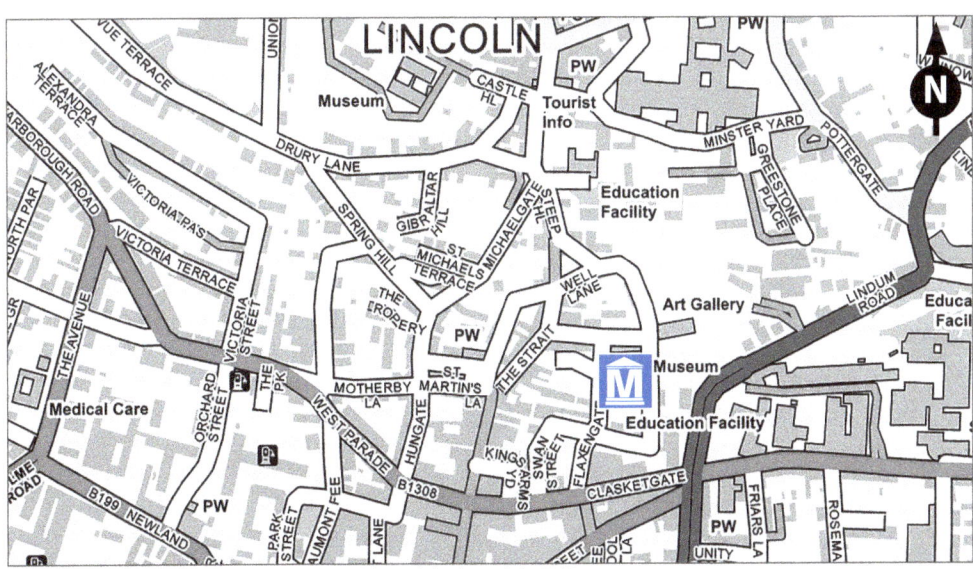

A speculative view of a Roman woman wearing the Horse Brooch and bone hairpin around 300 CE.

The Horse Brooch

In 2020 a metal detectorist unearthed an exceptionally rare and beautiful brooch in a field near Leasingham, a village about 20 miles *(32 km)* south of Lincoln. The brooch is a miniature version of a horse, made from copper alloy and perhaps was originally decorated with patterns of turquoise-coloured enamel.

The person who owned the brooch may have worn it to pin an outdoor cloak into place, securing it with the hinged pin. It would have been a treasured possession because of its exquisite workmanship and unusual design. Although horse brooches were a popular choice in Roman Britain, they were usually flat designs. The Romans used many different types of brooch to fasten their clothes, similar to the way we would use a safety-pin. Other animal-themed brooches found in Lincoln include a greyhound.

Find out more

The Horse Brooch is on permanent display in the Lincoln Museum, together with other animal-themed brooches in the collection. Also shown on the main image is a bone hairpin, found in Lincoln and on display in the Lincoln Museum.

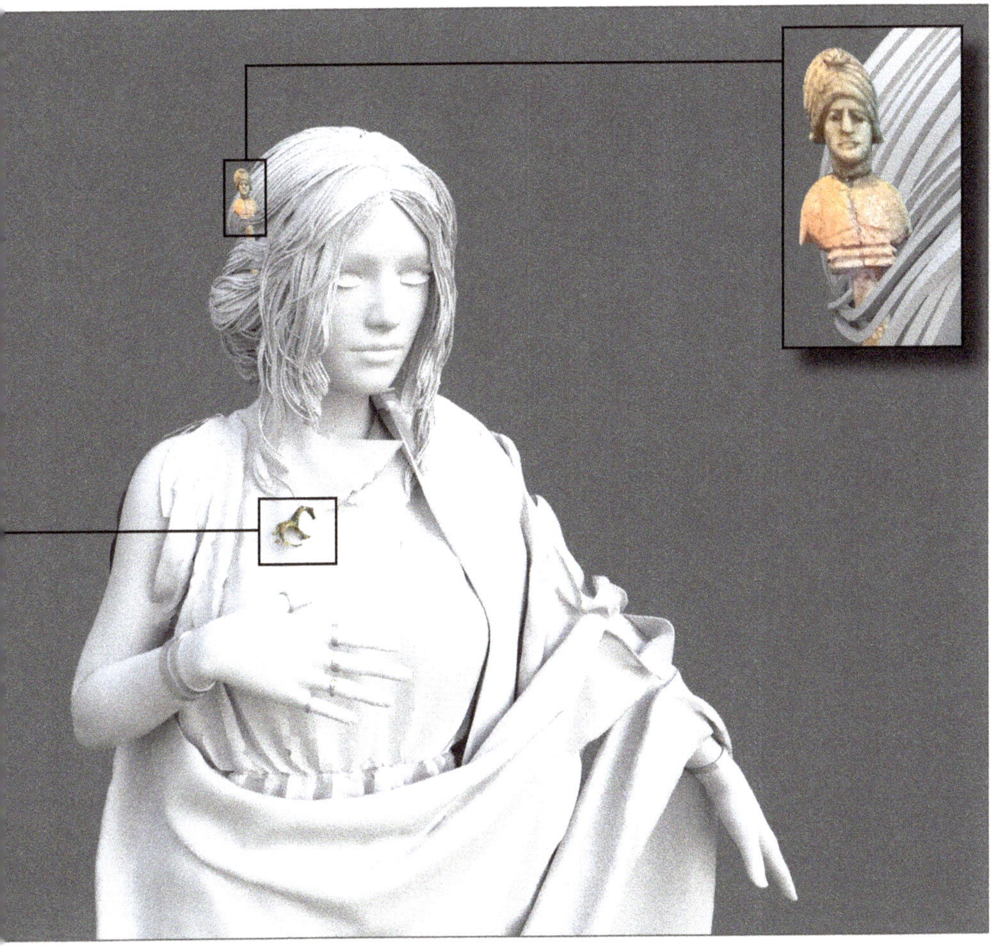

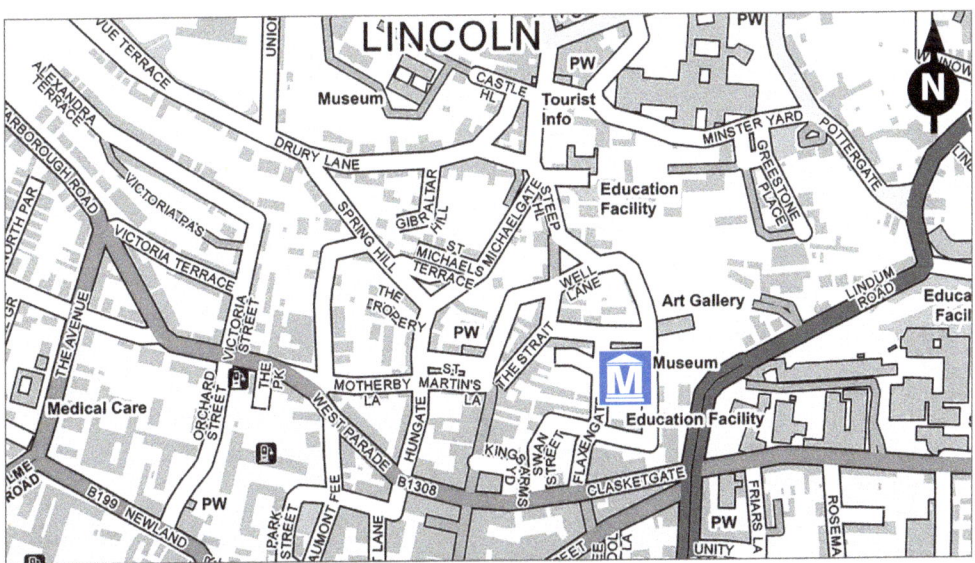

A possible interior of the villa which housed the Horkstow Mosaic, 360 CE.

The Horkstow Mosaic

Workmen constructing a kitchen garden at Horkstow Hall, 38 miles *(61 km)* north of Lincoln, in 1797 uncovered a spectacular mosaic, which was part of a Roman villa. The mosaic, about 15 metres long *(49 feet)*, was made in the mid-fourth century and would have decorated the main hall of the villa. There are three panels. The first of these panels features *Orpheus*[1], the second depicts popular classical themes[2] and the third is unique, with vivid imagery of scenes from a chariot race.

1. Orpheus was a legendary character from Greek mythology who travelled to the underworld to try to save his wife Eurydice. He was able to charm anything alive with his lyre (a small harp).
2. This panel called the 'Painted Ceiling' may show Achilles, a great warrior in the Trojan War or possibly Bacchus the God of Wine. The corners feature serpent-legged giants.

Find out more

The Horkstow Mosaic can be seen at the Hull and East Riding Museum 48 miles (77 km) north of Lincoln. Samuel Lysons, an antiquarian, produced detailed illustrations of the Horkstow mosaic and villa excavations, which are on display in the Lincoln Museum. The main image shows 10 Lectus Triclinaris (couches) allowing diners to eat and lie down. Mosaics in Spain show 15 diners all seated around one room in a similar fashion.

A view showing how much of the mosaic can be seen at the Hull and East Riding Museum.

Roman Lincoln today

Lindum Colonia lies under present day Lincoln city centre. Most of the visible Roman sites lie near to the castle and cathedral. The sites shown on this map are also explored in more detail in the main part of this book. All the exterior images of Roman Lincoln face north, so that you can compare the past with the present day maps.
The Lincoln Museum *(shown with a blue square)* has multiple Roman artefacts including:
The Fortuna Mosaic (page 22),
The Townhouse Mosaic (page 24),
The Ninth Legion (page 26),
The Horse Brooch (page 28),
The Horkstow Mosaic (page 30)

Key

Outlines of Roman walls
(still visible)

Outlines of Roman walls
(no longer visible)

Roman sites
(still visible)
12

Roman sites
(no longer visible)
12

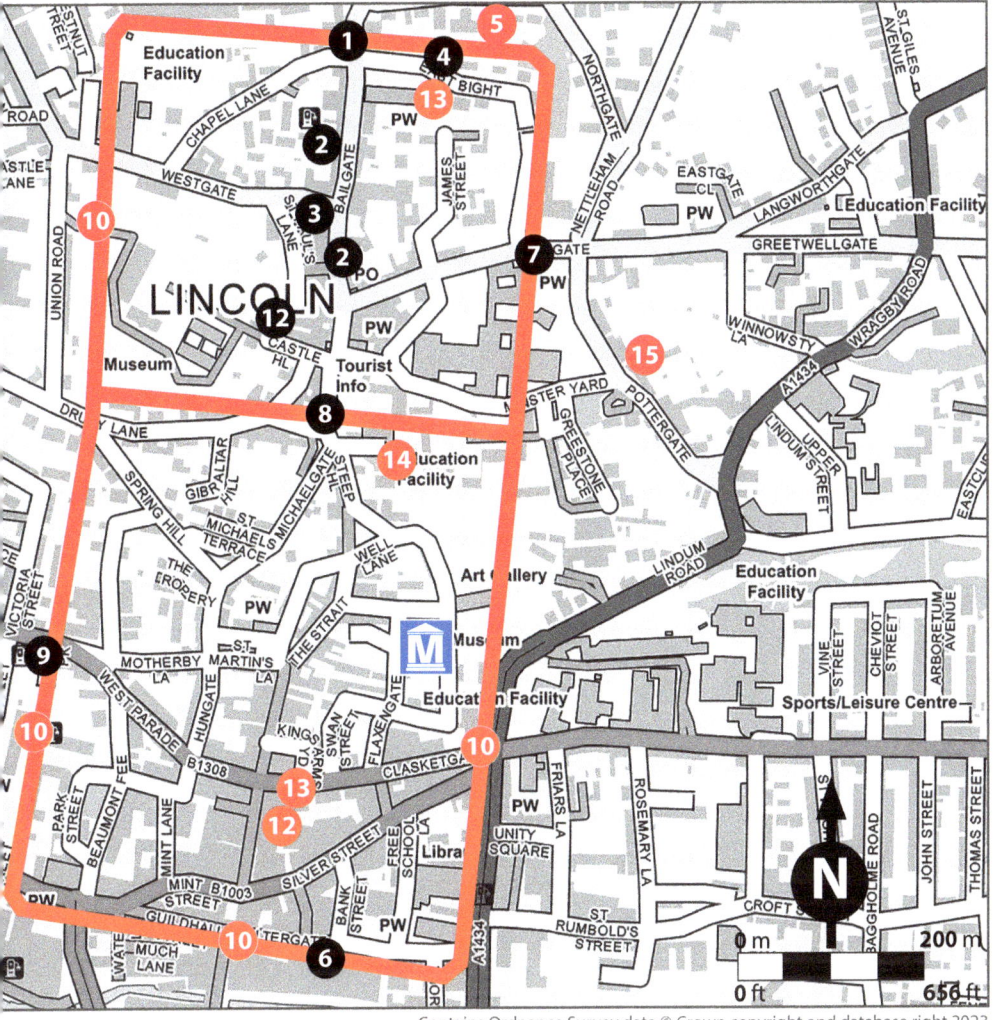

1. Newport Arch
(See page 18)

2. Forum and Basilica
(including Mint Wall)
(See page 20)

3. Legionary Fortress Well
(See page 12)

4. Water tank
(See page 20)

5. Aqueduct
(See page 20)

6. Posterngate
(See page 16)

7. Upper Eastgate
(See page 14)

8. Upper Southgate
(See page 14)

9. Lower Westgate
(See page 16)

10. Other Roman Gatehouses
(See page 10)

11. Fossdyke canal
(See page 8)

12. Temples
(See pages 14/16)

13. Public bathhouses
(See pages 114/16)

14. Theatre
(See page 14)

15. Amphitheatre
Conjectural location
(See page 14)

First published October 2023
ISBN 978-1-7391254-3-1 *(Paperback)*
First Edition

Designed and published by JC3DVIS
www.jc3dvis.co.uk
Book design © 2023 Joseph Chittenden

All the images in this guide were produced by JC3DVIS. Contains Ordnance Survey data © Crown copyright and database right 2023

The moral right of the copyright holder has been asserted.

All rights reserved. No part of this publication may be reproduced, distributed or transmitted in any form or by any means, including photocopying, recording, or other electronic or mechanical methods, without the prior written permission of the publisher.

With special thanks to:
Jane Chittenden *(written content, proof-reading)*

Legal disclaimer
Neither the author nor the publisher shall be held liable or responsible to any person or entity with respect to any loss or incidental or consequential damages caused, or alleged to have been caused, directly or indirectly, by the information contained herein.